MICHAEL EISNER

*Fun
for
Everyone*

D1607023

MICHAEL EISNER

Fun
for
Everyone

Sherill Tippins

GEC **GARRETT EDUCATIONAL CORPORATION**

Cover photo: *Michael Eisner.* **(Bonnie Schiffman/Onyx.)**

Manufactured in the United States of America

Edited and produced by Synthegraphics Corporation

Library of Congress Cataloging in Publication Data

Tippins, Sherill.
  Michael Eisner : fun for everyone / Sherill Tippins.
    p. cm. — (Wizards of business)
  Includes index.
  Summary: A biography of the highest-paid chief executive officer
in the United States, formerly vice president of ABC and president
of Paramount Pictures, and currently chairman of Walt Disney
Productions.
  ISBN 1-56074-014-0
  1. Eisner, Michael, 1942-   —Juvenile literature.   2. Walt Disney
Company—History—Juvenile literature.   3. Walt Disney Productions—
Reorganization—Juvenile literature.   4. Chief executive officers—
United States—Biography—Juvenile literature.   5. Motion picture
industry—United States—Biography—Juvenile literature.
[1. Eisner, Michael, 1942-   . 2. Chief executive officers.
3. Walt Disney Productions.]   I. Title.   II. Series.
PN1998.3.E36T66   1991
384′.8′092—dc20   91-28544
[B]   CIP
                                                               AC

Contents

Chronology for **Michael Eisner**   **6**

Chapter **1** *Wanted: Dreamer—Experience Preferred*   **7**

Chapter **2** *The Prince of Park Avenue*   **13**

Chapter **3** *Climbing the Ladder*   **20**

Chapter **4** *Teamwork Is the Key*   **26**

Chapter **5** *Outrageous Fortune*   **38**

Chapter **6** *Futureworld*   **46**

Chapter **7** *Dreams Can Come True*   **56**

Glossary   **61**

Index   **63**

Chronology for **Michael Eisner**

1942	Born in Mount Kisco, New York
1964	Graduated from Denison University
1966	Hired as an assistant at ABC-TV
1967	Married Jane Breckenridge
1968	Became vice-president for daytime programs at ABC-TV
1973	Made senior vice-president in charge of prime-time production at ABC-TV
1976	Became president of Paramount Pictures
1984	Appointed chairman of Walt Disney Productions
1986	Disney's profits doubled since Eisner's arrival
1988	Disney Studios achieved first place among the six major film studios
1989	Disney-MGM Studios Theme Park opened; Eisner was the highest paid chief executive officer in the United States
1990	Disney became world's most valuable entertainment company; Eisner began plans for EuroDisney

Chapter 1

Wanted: Dreamer— Experience Preferred

It was seven o'clock on an autumn evening in New York City. The streetlamps had just come on, bathing the crowded sidewalks in a golden glow. From a window in an elegant apartment house high above Park Avenue, nine-year-old Michael Dammann Eisner watched the action on the street in utter fascination. His sharp eyes had already picked out an interesting-looking couple talking on the corner below. They were elegantly dressed. The woman was very pretty.

Suddenly, the woman turned and quickly walked away. *She didn't even look back,* the boy thought. *Were they fighting?* He watched the man closely to see if he was observing the woman's departure. *He's not even watching her. I know, they're spies! That man just passed her an envelope full of military secrets.*

"Michael, come to supper!"

No, no! This guy's no spy! He's a cat burglar. The pretty woman is his partner. They're going to meet later at a party and take everyone's jewels.

"Michael! Supper's ready."

No, that can't be right. Michael looked down into the puddle of light beneath the streetlamp. The man was pacing back and forth. *They didn't meet by accident. They're planning something secret. But she has to talk with someone else first. They're going to meet here and then they're running away together. Running away from someone who . . .*

"Michael Eisner! Come to supper! *Now!*"

Michael's mother was standing less than ten feet from her son, sighing. *He's daydreaming again,* she thought to herself. Finally, she grasped him by the arm and half-dragged the boy to the dinner table.

"For heaven's sake, Michael," his mother complained as they joined Michael's father, a lawyer, and his older brother in the elegant, antique-filled dining room. "They're only ordinary people out there. When will you stop making a drama out of everything you see?"

The answer, if Mrs. Eisner had only known it, was *never.* In fact, it would be Michael Eisner's unusual imagination, coupled with his love of adventure and an unusual talent for knowing what people will buy, that would earn him a reputation as one of Hollywood's youngest whiz kids by the time he was thirty-four. When television networks and movie studios found themselves on the brink of **bankruptcy,** Michael Eisner soon became the man they would try to hire. (Terms in **boldface type** are defined in the Glossary at the back of this book.)

Michael had an understanding of what made people tick—gained from having studied them constantly from his living room window as a child. He also had a talent for finding successful new shows that would push TV networks and film studios past their competition. It was the combination of these unique abilities that propelled Michael Eisner straight to the top of nearly every company he would work for.

THE GREATEST CHALLENGE

Now it was 1984. At age forty-two, Michael was the very grown-up president of Paramount Pictures, one of Hollywood's largest movie studios. He was, however, still very much a boy at heart.

As he stood gazing out the living room window of his Beverly Hills mansion, Michael was pondering whether to accept the greatest show business challenge of his life. He had just been offered the job of his dreams: the chance to take over as head of Walt Disney Productions.

As everyone in Hollywood knew, Walt Disney Productions, which included Disney Studios, Disneyland, and Disneyworld, was in serious financial trouble. Since the death of its founder, Walt Disney, in 1966, the company had slid downhill fast and was now in danger of disappearing altogether. The company's management had frantically searched Hollywood for someone to take over Disney Productions before it was destroyed. Last night, they had offered Michael Eisner the job.

A Perfect Match

Michael Eisner had always loved Disney and his company. From its whimsical Mickey Mouse cartoons to its elaborate **theme parks,** the **conglomerate** Walt Disney had created in the 1940s was a company after Michael's own heart. Michael's boyish optimism, boundless energy, and wild imagination seemed a perfect match for the company that children loved most. And as the father of three sons, he had a special desire to see Disney survive for at least another generation.

Gazing out the window, Michael's mind was already churning with ideas, just as it did when he was nine years old. He could almost see the wonderful movies and the amazing theme park extravaganzas he'd invent as the head of Disney. But could he succeed in turning the run-down company around?

Behind him on the coffee table was a stack of financial papers showing just how much had gone wrong at Disney in the nearly twenty years since Walt Disney's death. Though the people who had taken over the company had respected and loved Mr. Disney, and were proud of the Disney name, none of them had had the imagination and daring of the company's founder.

The result was that Disney had just copied its own ideas for almost two decades, coming up with very few exciting new movies, cartoon characters, or rides. All across America, Disney products were beginning to have a reputation for being old-fashioned or silly. It was as if the Disney company was an old manual typewriter, trying to keep up with the modern computers that were the other movie studios and amusement parks.

It would take superhuman energy to save the company from sinking completely—energy Michael knew he had. In his twenties, that energy had helped make ABC Television number one among the three major television networks. In his thirties, his nose for a good screenplay had made Paramount Pictures the most successful film studio in Hollywood.

A Different Kind of Company

But Walt Disney Productions wasn't just a movie studio. It also included a record company, a television production company, an **animation** department, and more. It's theme parks—Disneyland, Disneyworld, and Epcot Center—were perhaps even more important than its movies. Each of these divisions was capable of earning a great deal of money. But they had all been neglected so much that most of them were losing money instead. The theme parks alone were expensive enough to bring the company down if they didn't attract enough visitors. However, much as Michael loved a good roller-coaster ride, he had to admit he knew nothing about the practical side of running an amusement park.

Saving Disney would take more than good entertainment instincts. The company had so little money to spend that saving it would take a combination of a strict, hard-headed sense for business and an ability to organize entire divisions. Also needed would be all the enthusiasm, wild ideas, and risk-taking ability that Walt Disney had put into it when he started Disney fifty years ago.

A DREAM COME TRUE

With his boyish enthusiasm and love of show business, Michael was excited by the idea of trying to fill the shoes of one of Hollywood's greatest geniuses. But did he have the business sense to run an enormous and complex company—and to force roller coasters to pay their way?

Michael glanced at his reflection in the window. He saw his

round, youthful face, lanky build and enthusiastic, puppy-like expression. Michael knew he looked an awful lot like a cross between Huckleberry Finn and one of the Disney movie's nutty professors.

Well, Michael sighed as he turned away from the window, *it isn't going to be easy.* But he knew that rescuing the best-loved company in show business was too great a challenge to turn down. And Michael also knew, in his heart of hearts, that having control of a company as exciting as Disney was the dream of a lifetime come true.

Chapter 2

The Prince of Park Avenue

When reporters once asked Michael Eisner why his entertainment ideas for American audiences were so often enjoyed by so many people, he told them it was mostly luck.

THE BABY-BOOM GENERATION

Born in Mount Kisco, New York, in 1942, Michael appeared right at the start of America's baby boom—the largest number of babies ever born in the United States. That meant that hundreds of thousands of children growing up in America happened to be the same age as Michael.

And chances were that as he grew up, whatever Michael happened to be interested in at a particular time—teenage romance, for example, or marriage and family life—was usually the same thing that those hundreds of thousands of other Americans his age were just becoming interested in, too.

As a typical American guy, all Michael had to do, he believed, was follow his own developing fascinations. And most of the baby boomers—the biggest **market** share in America, whom advertisers wanted most to reach—would follow right along.

Market Share

In television, the word "market" simply means the people watching television. A "market share" is the number and type of people who usually watch a particular television show.

It is important for advertisers to know what sort of people watch a particular TV show because they want their commercials to play for the most appropriate audience. For example, a television soap opera's market share includes mostly women between the ages of eighteen and thirty-five who don't work outside the home. Therefore, companies that make kitchen appliances or cleaning supplies would want to advertise on that show, but companies that manufacture pickup trucks would not.

Television broadcasting companies make most of their income from television commercials. That's why it is important for them to produce television shows that attract the best market share. The best market share, as far as most advertisers are concerned, is the share that is the largest. It is also the share that is willing and able to spend the most money.

By keeping track of who buys their clients' products, advertisers have learned over the years that baby boomers often like to spend money, and have more money to spend, than people older or younger than they are. There are also more baby boomers than there are of any other group in America. That makes them a favorite market share for television commercials.

A television company whose shows attract baby-boom viewers will be able to sell more commercial time, at higher prices, to advertisers. That is why a baby-boom market share is a very valuable **asset.**

Inspiration from Books

Another lucky accident was that Michael was born into a family that believed in the value of a good education. Michael was sent to some of the best private schools in the country. At these schools, he read most of the greatest books written in the English language.

At home, Michael's father only allowed his children to watch television if they read two hours for every hour of TV. Thus, Michael read more stories and books than most kids.

All of those stories, stored in the back of his head, would later help Michael see what was wrong with a failing television show.

They would also help him choose the best movie scripts for his companies. In fact, several of Michael's most successful ideas for movies were directly inspired by the old classics he'd read as a boy.

Learning Business Concepts

A third bit of luck was that business matters were often discussed over dinner at Michael's house. And his parents would include him in the conversation.

Michael's grandfather had founded the American Safety Razor Company, which he sold for a fortune after he retired. Michael's father was a successful New York City attorney. His income, along with the money from the razor company, enabled the family to live in the elegant Park Avenue apartment from whose windows Michael liked to study human nature.

Michael was a bright boy who kept his ears open. He picked up business concepts from his family as naturally as he learned table manners. And from his father he learned not only the value but the joy of being a tough **negotiator.**

Michael's love of books made him wonder, as he grew up, whether he'd like to become a writer. While attending Denison University, a small college in Ohio, he tried writing a few plays— mostly to impress a pretty classmate. But, as his professors pointed out, Michael really preferred *talking* about ideas rather than working alone at a desk.

The friendly, outgoing nineteen-year-old soon realized that a writing life was too lonely for him. He matter-of-factly decided he'd better go into business instead, where he could put his skills as a captivating talker to good use.

FIRST STEPS

Michael soon discovered that the business he enjoyed most was show business. Assigned a small part in a college play, he found himself attracted to the loose, friendly atmosphere backstage. He liked discussing the play with the rest of the cast, and talking about great ideas for plays not yet written.

Michael decided that a career among creative people like these was exactly what would make him happy. Though his grades were never spectacular, Michael managed to talk his way into a summer job as a page at NBC Television after his junior year in college.

Following his graduation from Denison in 1964, Michael took a job as a clerk at NBC. There, his enthusiasm and never-ending curiosity encouraged others to teach him all they knew about the business of producing TV shows.

Adventures in Television

It wasn't long before Michael won his first promising job. In 1966, Ted Fedder, vice-president and national **program director** of ABC-TV, hired the twenty-four-year-old as an assistant. Michael couldn't believe he was actually working in show business so soon. He was now talking with real writers, directors, and producers, even if he was only delivering messages from his powerful boss.

Michael watched Fedder like a hawk. He studied the way the man decided what shows would best capture the television audience's attention. He saw that daytime television depended mostly on soap operas. The cliffhanger endings and long, drawn-out plots of the soaps were designed to keep the audience tuning in day after day. Michael also learned that most of ABC's evening programming was based on comedies and police shows that had been on for years, and that had always attracted viewers.

Recognizing a Problem

But as he watched and learned, Michael began to think that, as a younger man, he might have some better, more up-to-date ideas for programs himself. Many of ABC's shows seemed boring and old-fashioned to him. In the 1960s, styles were changing fast, yet ABC's television shows seemed stuck in the 1950s. As Michael experienced a typical lifestyle for a young man in his twenties—dating, working hard at a career, and sometimes longing for his simpler high school days—he wondered why his concerns weren't reflected in the TV shows he saw.

If there was a funny series on TV about dating in America, Michael thought, *he* would certainly watch it! And if the soap opera stories were more shocking, wouldn't young people be more likely to tune in! The problem with ABC's TV shows, he finally decided, was that they just weren't "cool."

Michael's constant questions and suggestions soon caught the attention of the more powerful executives in the company. ABC was sinking fast in the ratings. In fact, the network was in last place behind CBS and NBC. Maybe the people in charge of choosing which shows were aired really *were* too old-fashioned, as Michael Eisner thought.

Already, baby-boomers—that big-spending group of Americans who were now in their early twenties—had become the most desirable television audience. Advertisers who paid a lot of money to the three networks wanted baby-boomers to see their TV commercials. That was why, if the baby-boomers didn't like a show, the show soon died.

THE "DYNAMIC DUO"

The top executives of ABC took a long look at young Michael Eisner. He never stopped chattering about what baby-boomers would rather see on TV. Maybe he knew what he was talking about, they decided. Maybe ABC's programming *wasn't* "cool" enough.

Being in last place, the ABC-TV executives had little to lose. They decided to take a chance on the aggressive, ambitious young man and his wild, imaginative ideas. So, only two years after he arrived at ABC, Michael was promoted to vice-president for daytime programs, making him, at age 27, one of the two youngest vice-presidents in the network's history.

The other young vice-president was Barry Diller, another baby-boomer. Diller would soon become Michael's friend and companion in modernizing ABC. Within months, people were calling the two the "dynamic duo."

Chapter 3

Climbing the Ladder

Michael knew he was extraordinarily lucky to be given a chance to prove himself at such a young age. Newly married in 1967 to Jane Breckenridge and anxious to make his mark at ABC, he spent twelve to fifteen hours a day figuring out why so few people watched the network's daytime shows.

Every moment he was awake Michael studied the scripts of ABC's soap operas. He also went over proposals for new shows and watched the other TV channels to see what the competition was doing. What did the other networks have that ABC didn't have, Michael asked himself? What could he put on his network that *he* would want to see? How could he improve the company's ratings?

Ratings

"Ratings" is the measurement of how many people are watching a particular television show. The rating for a show is measured by finding out how many people in several small areas across the country are watching the show, and then averaging the number for the country as a whole.

Ratings are important to a television company because of their value in attracting advertisers. The more people who watch a particular show (that is, the higher the show's ratings are), the more people advertisers can reach with television commercials on that show. The higher the ratings, the more valuable that show is to advertisers. When a show is valuable, the television company can charge advertisers more money for putting their commercials on it. And the more money the television company charges, the greater its **income** is.

Television companies measure their success almost wholly on how high their ratings are for all their shows. The company with the highest combined ratings is the most successful company for that season. It is paid more money than other TV companies for its commercials.

SPICING UP THE SOAPS

Michael decided that the trouble with ABC's soap operas was that they were just too tame. The things that shocked and fascinated viewers ten years ago didn't keep the attention of younger viewers. The shows needed characters who were really wild or evil or both, and plots to match.

Michael started using his writing experience to "punch up"

the plots of the network's soaps. He added scandals and more intrigue to the plots so that viewers would keep watching the ABC-TV programs day after day.

Michael also added new, fast-paced quiz shows that offered magnificent prizes, and he broadcast some popular old comedy shows that he himself would like to see again. Annoyed by viewers' habit of switching channels after every show, he also developed a series of longer TV dramas to keep viewers tuned in for an hour or more.

A Creative Worker

Michael was not a loner. He liked working creatively with other people and would often talk his ideas over with his co-worker, Barry Diller. The two young men enjoyed brainstorming together— it made coming up with ideas even more fun. And since they were the same age, Michael and Barry usually agreed that their ideas were brilliant.

After a particularly productive brainstorming session, Barry and Michael would reassure each other that if *they* were watching the new bunch of shows they had just dreamed up, they would never switch channels. They were sure that the television audience, most of them their own age or a little younger, would feel the same way.

Soon after Michael set to work, ABC's daytime ratings began to rise. By 1973, ABC was first in daytime ratings, and the credit went to the "dynamic duo." Word in the show business community was out: Eisner's and Diller's daring ideas turned troubled entertainment companies into solid winners.

By putting his own ideas, enthusiasm, and energy to work,

Michael had faced his first challenge in the entertainment business and had won.

NEW IDEAS, NEW SHOWS

In 1973, Michael was made senior vice-president in charge of **prime-time** production at ABC. Now he had the chance to develop the ideas for shows that had been crowding his imagination since his days as a beginning assistant. One after another, Michael developed a series of TV hits based on those ideas.

The hits included *Love, American Style, Happy Days, Laverne and Shirley,* and *Charlie's Angels.* These were all shows that Michael liked himself, and that he believed people his age would enjoy, too. He also explored his idea for producing made-for-TV movies, and proved how right he was by developing the spectacularly successful mini-series, *Roots.*

By 1976, Michael—now thirty-four years old—had performed his own personal brand of show business miracle for the second time. ABC's prime-time schedule, once at the bottom of the network rankings, was now number one. Michael seemed to have a golden touch where predicting audience taste was concerned. He was sure to receive another promotion. This time, however, what he received was a better offer from another company.

MOVING ON

In 1976, Michael's old friend and co-worker, Barry Diller, had been hired as chairman of Paramount Pictures in Los Angeles, California. As soon as he could, Barry offered Michael the job of president of Paramount.

Both men were quite similar in many respects. Both were team players. They liked to come up with ideas by locking themselves in a room and brainstorming for hours. They also insisted on overseeing all of their projects personally from beginning to end.

Paramount Pictures was in last place among the six major Hollywood studios. Barry knew he needed Michael's unbelievable energy, enthusiasm, and instinct for spotting a money-making story to turn the movie studio around.

A Talent for Success

Michael was delighted to take the new job. He loved nothing more than the challenge of reorganizing a company and making it work right. And Barry knew that a man as friendly and eager as Michael Eisner would be well liked by Hollywood's writers, actors, and directors.

Barry was right. Michael had a talent for turning any group of people he worked with into an enthusiastic team. Repeating their earlier successes at ABC-TV, the dynamic duo of Diller and Eisner were responsible for such Paramount movie smashes as *Saturday Night Fever, Grease, Heaven Can Wait, Raiders of the Lost Ark,* and *Reds.* They were also responsible for such popular Paramount television series as "Mork and Mindy" and "Taxi." Show business people such as Stephen Spielberg, Warren Beatty, and Robin Williams loved Michael because he was as fun-loving as they were, and because he believed the quality of a film was as important as how much money it made. Movie executives admired Michael because, with Barry Diller, he had made Paramount number one among the six major Hollywood studios in just a few years.

THE GREATEST CHALLENGE OF ALL

But now it was 1984. The challenge of turning Paramount around was over and Michael felt restless. He longed for new worlds to conquer—he wanted to prove himself again somewhere else. Not only that, but this time he wanted to control not just the choice of shows but the whole company. He wanted to see what would happen if he ran an entire organization his way.

But at Walt Disney Productions? Over the past ten years, Hollywood's other film studios had left Disney's old-fashioned movies in the dust, and nobody thought of Disneyland as new and exciting any more. If Michael had to pick the most difficult company in Hollywood to save, Disney would win by a mile.

On the other hand, no company in Hollywood needed a knight in shining armor more than Walt Disney Productions. If Eisner took over the reins, he could make show business history. *If* he was successful, that is. *If* he could take a money-losing movie studio, a few run-down amusement parks, and a collection of old cartoons and turn them into something truly magic.

Disney's management made Michael an offer. If he wanted to run the famous company, it was his for the taking. All Hollywood awaited Michael's decision.

Chapter 4

Teamwork Is the Key

On September 22, 1984, Michael Eisner became chairman of Walt Disney Productions. But he was smart enough to know he would need some serious help in getting the ailing company back on its feet. And Michael had never been slow to ask for help when he needed it.

REBUILDING THE MAGIC KINGDOM

To assist him with the business aspects of the company, Michael hired an old Hollywood friend, Frank Wells, as president. Wells was a big-time Hollywood lawyer who had a reputation as being a genius with business negotiations and contracts. The two men agreed that at Disney, Michael would act as the scout for creative new ideas, while Frank, who was much more experienced in business practices, would decide whether the company could afford them.

Michael Eisner, the head of Walt Disney Productions, with some of the famous Disney characters known to children and adults throughout the world. (Aaron Rapoport/Onyx.)

The people at Disney liked the familiar feel of this two-person team. It reminded them of Walt Disney himself, who had concentrated on creative ideas while his brother, Roy, took care of the company's budget, expenses, and investments. That creative/practical team had worked brilliantly until Walt's death in 1966. Now, Disney's management hoped Michael's similar set-up would work as well again.

Putting a Team Together

On September 23, the day after they started working at Disney, Michael and Frank found themselves wandering the corridors of Walt Disney's historic animation building on the studio lot. Michael could hardly contain his excitement. Walt Disney himself had always worked in this humble three-story building, alongside his fellow cartoonists, and now his old office belonged to Michael. *If I had known when I was a kid that I'd have the chance to run Disney,* Michael thought with a smile, *I'd have died of impatience waiting for it to happen.*

Stepping into Disney's shoes, though, wasn't going to be all fun and games for Michael. What had started as a simple cartoon production company was now a messy collection of failing divisions, almost all of them losing money fast. Reading the company's financial reports, Frank Wells had told him, was like looking at the remains of a beautiful Rolls Royce that had been left to fall into separate piles of rusting metal beside a deserted highway.

Putting the parts back together and getting them to work as a powerful unit would take years, Michael realized. But he had no intention of spending those years alone. He wisely set to work putting together a top-of-the line, ambitious, and creative group of show business executives to head Disney's various departments and make up the new Disney team. A happy, creative team made happy, creative products, Michael reasoned. Besides, it was more fun working together on projects than toiling away on one's own.

Taking Time for Family

Most of the people Michael hired were baby-boomers like himself who had married and were starting their families. Michael believed it was important for employees of a family-oriented company like

Disney to be involved in family life themselves. He himself occasionally walked out of high-level meetings to attend an Indian Scout meeting with one of his three sons. And every Saturday he appeared to cheer them on at one of their sports events.

Michael not only valued the time he spent with his children, he also knew he needed to keep in touch with what kids talked about these days, and what concerned them. Later, he would even get ideas for Disney from his own growing boys. The idea for the Saturday morning cartoon show, *The Adventures of the Gummi Bears,* hit him while he was buying his youngest son's favorite candy.

The hardworking parents at Disney soon found that spending Saturday mornings watching cartoons with their kids served several purposes. It not only made their kids like them better. It also got the parents excited about their work as well.

The Gong Show

Michael and Frank did their best to encourage the Disney employees to feel free to come up with all kinds of ideas, even if they seemed stupid. Everyone on what Michael and Frank called "Team Disney" was encouraged to share passing interests and to constructively criticize everyone else's ideas as well—even Michael's.

After his second week at Disney, Michael started a series of Sunday-morning meetings at his mansion in Beverly Hills. The meetings were called "gong shows." Michael would lock himself up in a room with several of his employees for several hours while everyone bounced ideas off everyone else. If an idea didn't seem realistic to the others, they had the right to "gong" it out of existence—even if the idea was Michael's.

Michael was famous for his wacky ideas. His description of a skyscraper hotel shaped like Mickey Mouse was one of the first proposals to be gonged. It was a relief to his employees to discover that Michael had enough of a sense of humor about himself to be teased out of enacting his wilder notions.

The method worked best if no refreshments were served, Michael soon discovered. Hollywood executives would say all kinds of brilliant things on a Sunday morning if they knew that afterwards they'd be let out to eat!

Teamwork Throughout the Company

During his first months at Disney, Michael emphasized over and over that this kind of teamwork was the key to saving the company. He stressed the need for teamwork not only between creative employees but between different departments as well. Michael planned, for example, to produce animated films at Disney whose characters would then be sold as stuffed animals, action figures, and Disneyland characters. The music from these films would be sold as records. And the themes of the films would not only be turned into television cartoons, they would also inspire new rides and pavilions at the theme parks, Disneyland in California and Disneyworld and Epcot Center in Florida.

Alone, each division might make a respectable amount of money. But Disney owned properties in nearly every area of entertainment, from classic children's films to land for Disney resorts. Michael's mission, he believed, was to make the separate parts work together superbly well. Only in that way would this old Rolls Royce be able to take to the highways again in regal splendor.

FUELING DISNEY'S ENGINE

First, though, Michael had to generate enough **cash flow** so that he could put his favorite projects in motion. During his first week at Disney, he looked at the theme parks and discovered that their admission prices were much too low. Before his arrival, Disney management had refused to raise the prices because they feared such an act would discourage tourists and would make the company look bad.

Michael thought that was ridiculous. Just a dollar increase in admission prices could increase the theme parks' profits by millions every year, so this simple act was an important first step. He ordered that the admission prices be raised gradually over several years. This income would provide the money to power most of Disney's first projects under Michael's leadership.

Rescuing Disney Studios

Next, Michael turned to his pet division, movies. What he found was shocking. Disney Studios and its subdivision, Touchstone Pictures, had been losing money for the past three years. And Michael could see that the few projects in progress were probably money-losers, too. So he scrapped them all and set to work deciding how to start over.

At that time, the average film in Hollywood cost around $18 million to produce. This did not include advertising and such other post-production expenses as making copies of the film for theaters, printing posters, and the like. Because Disney didn't have that kind of money to spend, Michael wondered at first how he would ever pull the studio out of its downward fall.

Then he came up with a brilliant idea. Michael remembered that there was one thing actors and directors like even more than money—a good story for them to act in or direct.

So, instead of spending what little money Disney had on expensive star actors and directors, the way most studios did to guarantee themselves huge **profits,** Michael told his employees to concentrate on finding strong, modern, entertaining screenplays. With a really good screenplay, Michael insisted, actors would agree to work even if the pay were lower than usual. And anyway, a movie with a good story would succeed no matter who the actors or directors were.

Michael and the rest of Team Disney then made a list of well-known movie stars who had the talent but who hadn't been lucky enough to have had a hit recently. The list included such performers as Bette Midler, Robin Williams, and Danny De Vito. Michael reasoned that such actors would be most likely to work at bargain-basement salaries because of the excellent screenplays Disney now owned.

Disney Studios was in business once again. And Michael, along with the rest of Team Disney, held his breath for the two long years it would take to tell whether their plan had worked.

FINDING BURIED TREASURE

Even though he had found a possible way out of Disney's money-shortage problem, Michael knew that a basic lesson of business is that it takes money to make money. If he intended to produce good movies, TV shows, Disneyland attractions, and other products, he needed money to hire the best talent he could find. It was this search for instant cash that led him to Disney's enormous vaults of old movies, which contained such great children's films as *Snow White, Cinderella, Lady and the Tramp,* and *Peter Pan.*

Michael knew it was a Disney policy to show these movies every seven years in theaters around the country. He also knew that Disney's management had refused to sell them on videocassette. They were afraid that if people could buy the movies for viewing at home, they would stop coming to the theaters to see them over and over.

But Michael didn't believe that was true. He remembered how much he had loved reading his favorite books over and over as a child, and how much his own children enjoyed seeing the same show over and over on TV if they liked it enough. He believed that children who fell in love with these great movies at home would want to see them in the theaters even more.

To Michael, finding these rarely seen movies in Disney's vaults was like finding a treasure chest full of gold. He ordered that one or two of these wonderful movies be sold on videocassette every year at Christmas. The sales of these cassettes earned billions of dollars—money that Disney desperately needed for its other departments.

IMPROVING THE THEME PARKS

One of the departments at Walt Disney Productions that needed money most was the theme parks: Disneyland in Anaheim, California, and Disneyworld and Epcot Center in Orlando, Florida. Michael

Fireworks light up the night sky at Disneyworld in Orlando, Florida. Since Michael Eisner became the head of Disney Productions, attendance has increased at the company's theme parks due to many improvements as well as the addition of new rides and other features. (Ted Thai/Time Magazine.)

worried that the theme parks looked dated and shabby, especially now that he was charging more for people to visit them. He decided that what they needed was some up-to-date show business pizzazz to capture the attention of the public again.

Because of the Disney name associated with the theme parks, Michael wanted to hire the very best creative talent he could find. So he met with George Lucas, the producer of the hit movie, *Star Wars,* and asked him to design a new ride.

Star Tours and Captain EO

Like most artists Michael dealt with, Lucas had loved Disney as a child. He was thrilled at having a chance to contribute to a company that had given him so much joy. After thinking hard for a while, Lucas came up with something called Star Tours. It was a spaceship ride that combined the use of film, computers, and fantastic special effects. Even though the ride cost $32 million to make, it became a spectacular new favorite at Disneyland.

Team Disney loved Lucas' idea. It combined creative imagination with technological gadgetry that Walt Disney himself would have been amazed by. Inspired by Lucas' enthusiasm, the Disney team went on to convince Michael Jackson to make a seventeen-minute, 3-D movie musical called *Captain EO*. Produced by George Lucas, *Captain EO* set a new high for movie magic.

Ideas like the Star Tours ride and *Captain EO* film livened up the fading theme parks, giving tourists new reasons to visit them. New attractions also gave magazines and newspapers new reasons to write about Disney, and these articles provided free publicity for the struggling company.

Michael's sons offered their ideas for new rides, too. Splash Mountain, a $35-million giant log-roll ride to be built at Disneyland, was one son's idea, as was Typhoon Lagoon at Disneyworld.

In fact, Michael found to his surprise that running amusement parks was just the type of business that suited his playful personality. He began spending more and more time improving the parks and other Disney properties, paying attention to every last detail, as he was known to do and as Walt Disney had been known to do before him. Also like Disney, Michael could be spotted on the grounds of Disneyworld quite often just before dawn, picking up candy wrappers from the well-swept streets and dreaming up new ways to make Disney's parks the most irresistible entertainment in the world.

A NEW GENERATION OF DISNEY FANS

When he first arrived at Disney, Michael found that the company didn't have much of anything to sell, but he soon changed that. After developing the Gummi Bears TV series, he turned to Disney comics, which had been out of print in recent years.

At the time, America was experiencing a baby boomlet. Along with the Disney employees, most other baby-boom adults were finally getting around to having children. Michael developed a new comic books industry at Disney to take advantage of this new generation of readers. He also developed a new hit Saturday morning TV cartoon series, *DuckTales,* based on Donald Duck's three nephews and his Uncle Scrooge. And he quickly developed several comic book series featuring the same feathered rascals.

While he was introducing new comic books, Michael happened to learn that the Italian magazine, *Topolino,* was for sale. *Topolino* is the Italian name for Mickey Mouse. Michael bought the publication and made it the third best-selling magazine in that country. This success gave Michael his first hint that Disney's popularity was not something that was found just in the United States. Rather, it was a worldwide phenomenon.

Chapter 5

Outrageous Fortune

As it turned out, Michael was wise to take every bit of income he could from Disney's properties and **invest** it in new ideas. One reason was that, just as Michael took the helm at Disney, a large new audience of children—the offspring of the baby-boomers—was ready to be introduced to the Disney name for the first time. Another reason was that the nation's **economy** was booming, and Americans had more money to spend on entertainment.

FILM SUCCESSES

By 1985, as the first Disney movies under Michael's leadership began appearing in theaters, everything he touched seemed to be turning to gold. Team Disney's first two feature films, *Down and Out in Beverly Hills* and *Ruthless People,* both Touchstone releases, earned millions of dollars. They were the studio's first film successes in years and proved that Michael Eisner had not lost his talent for knowing a winning story when he saw one. Encouraged, Michael announced that the film department would release fifteen movies in 1987 and 1988, compared with the three or four a year produced before he arrived at Disney.

In 1987, *Outrageous Fortune,* starring Bette Midler, became another hit. And in 1988, Disney Studios' dreams really began to come true. *Three Men and a Baby* and *Good Morning, Vietnam* were both released that year and became back-to-back **blockbusters.** This was very important to both Michael and Disney Studios because blockbuster status means something extra special to Hollywood's show business industry. It also signalled to all of show business that Walt Disney Productions was back in the race, and that it would take more than run-of-the-mill competition to beat this up-and-coming company.

Other Successes

But the good news didn't end there. Children's movies had always been Disney's bread and butter, and thanks to Michael's involvement with his own sons, he was able to understand what types of films appealed to the younger generation.

Who Framed Roger Rabbit? was a Touchstone picture Michael loved so much that he broke his own low-budget rule and invested more than $40 million dollars in its production. The movie became the highest-**grossing** film of the year. Disney Studios also released *Oliver and Company,* another big hit with its fresh, young voices and modern music. Michael found it very satisfying to realize that, just as he had dreamed, a new generation was as thrilled with Disney as Michael himself had been.

Other departments at Walt Disney Productions were also doing very well. *Lady and the Tramp* had become the best-selling videotape of all time, and *DuckTales* was a TV hit. The Star Tours ride and *Captain EO* movie had opened at the theme parks and were whopping successes, raising park profits and bringing Disney into the news again. With his nose for a good TV show, Michael had bought the syndication rights to the TV hit, *Golden Girls.* The show's syndication promised to bring in more millions of dollars for Disney. And in 1987, more than a billion dollars' worth of Disney products were sold by the company's consumer products division.

Syndication

When you watch old *I Love Lucy* or *Dallas* episodes, you're watching a syndicated show. That means that your local TV station has purchased the right to run the show from a syndicator. A syndicator is a company that pays the producers of a show like *Dallas* for the right to sell reruns of the show to the thousands of local television stations across the country and around the world. Each time a television station airs the rerun, it must pay the owner of the syndication rights a certain amount of money.

Syndication rights are valuable because the shows have already been produced. No more money has to be spent making the shows. A company simply has to make one large payment for the syndication rights, and then earn hundreds of millions of dollars as each local TV station sends in money each time it broadcasts a tape of the show.

TURNING WEAKNESSES INTO STRENGTHS

Early on, Michael realized that one of Disney's greatest problems—its large size, with companies that produced everything from stuffed animals to feature films—was also its biggest advantage. The reason was that every new idea—say, a new cartoon show for Saturday morning TV—could also be used in the conglomerate's other departments.

This was in accordance with Michael's plan for teamwork between departments. Thus, the cartoon characters of the TV show could be sold as stuffed toys or might even inspire rides at Disneyland and Disneyworld. The show's theme songs could be sold on Disney records, and old shows in the series could be sold on videocassette. The characters might even inspire a full-length animated motion picture if they proved popular enough.

All of these products, developed from one new idea, could provide an enormous profit for Disney. That profit could be put to work **financing** even more daring and exciting ideas. Michael's insistence that every good idea be developed in every department of the company also meant that if one department did poorly in any one year, the other departments should be able to keep the company profitable.

MAKING MONEY FROM HIGH TECHNOLOGY

Michael borrowed another of his tricks for success from Walt Disney himself. In his time, Walt Disney had been famous for financing the most futuristic entertainment in the world. He wowed audiences not only with the superior detail and sound quality of his cartoons, but with the lifelike quality of his talking mannequins at Disneyland as well.

Disney Productions had always been equated with high technology in entertainment. And Michael was determined to keep it that way—letting Frank Wells worry about how much this high technology would cost.

In fact, improving the quality of Disney's products was one of the most enjoyable parts of Michael's job. He was just as enthusiastic over every new breakthrough in show business technology as Walt Disney had been.

Michael believed so much in the potential for Disney's new 3-D cameras that he insisted the company buy the **patents** for it. He also loved the lasers, fiber optics, and new technology for the mechanical figures at the theme parks. And he invested in a futuristic-sounding "Computer-Assisted Post-Production System" to save time and money creating the drawings for animated films and television cartoons.

Even the hotels Michael built later at Disneyworld required the most modern architecture and building technology available in the world. He sensed that his fascination with these showy gimmicks was shared by most other Americans. His sense was to prove correct as audiences flocked to experience the future—Disney style.

Cost Counts

Though he truly loved expensive machinery, Michael made sure that Frank Wells continued to keep a strict eye on the **bottom line.** Michael knew that many successful businesses fail when too much money is spent too quickly on future projects.

Michael also followed Wells' advice to find outside investors for riskier projects instead of taking a chance with the company's own **capital.** That way, if the project failed, Disney would not have lost any of its own money. But if the project succeeded, the company would be able to keep a part of the profits.

Michael also agreed with Walt Disney that the best advertising was free advertising. Michael worked to make joint promotions with other companies, such as McDonald's, in which the fast-food restaurant chain used Disney's animated characters as free giveaways in exchange for publicizing the characters' movies, such as *Oliver and Company,* free of charge.

But Michael also believed in paid advertising, and this was a major change for the company. Before Michael had arrived at Disney, management had spent almost nothing on advertising. But Michael, with his television experience, believed strongly in the value of television commercials. After he placed the first ads for Disneyworld on television, people began attending the park in even greater numbers.

"A TOUCH OF CLASS"

As Walt Disney had done before him, Michael worked hard to add "a touch of class" to every Disney project. These touches included using top movie producer George Lucas to design a Disney ride. They also included using Michael Graves, an internationally famous architect, to design the outrageous Swan Hotel and Dolphin Hotel that would soon grace the outside of Epcot Center.

Such touches of class brought attention to Disney. Articles

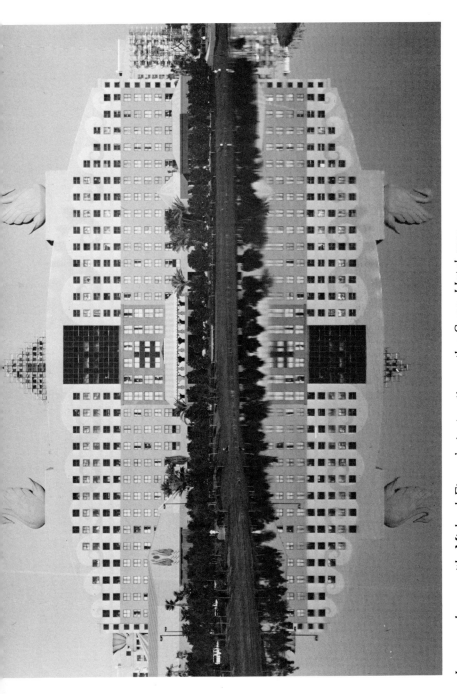

In accordance with Michael Eisner's instructions, the Swan Hotel was designed to add "a touch of class" outside of Epcot Center. (Michael Mundy.)

were written about Disneyworld each time a new ride or hotel was erected. Wilder and more imaginative rides and hotels with enormous dolphins carved into them led to a large number of TV news spots and newspaper articles about Disney. All this meant even more free advertising for the company. Disneyland and Disneyworld were new and exciting again, and that brought in new visitors by the thousands.

Chapter 6

Futureworld

Michael was certainly doing something right. By 1988, Disney's earnings had increased by more than 500 percent since 1984. Because of Eisner's way of developing each idea in every department, profitable Disney television cartoons led to profitable new comic books and stuffed animals, as well as new theme park attractions and sometimes new feature films. Almost every idea that was used at Disney led to an enormous explosion of profitable products.

THE SORCERER'S APPRENTICE

Some observers were reminded of the *Sorcerer's Apprentice,* a story that Disney had turned into a Mickey Mouse cartoon years before. In that story, the scorcerer's helper uses a magic broom to clean the wizard's workshop. The enchanted broom multiplies into more brooms, and more brooms, and even more brooms until the workshop is overwhelmed and chaos results.

As Michael tended Walt Disney's company, profits grew like the apprentice's brooms until it seemed there'd be no end. Michael himself became the highest paid **chief executive officer** in the United States, earning $40 million in 1988 alone.

Fortunately, though, Michael never lost control of his workshop. That was because he worked long, hard hours, studying the effects of his programs on the public and catching up on what the competition was doing. And he was careful to keep up his enthusiasm and creativity by spending time with his children.

Michael also kept an eagle eye on television, newspapers, magazines, new entertainments, and even such details of daily life as gummi bear candy. He did this in order to be able to spot new ideas that could help expand his empire. Michael also knew how to assign to assistants whom he respected and trusted work that he was too busy to handle. Thus, he was more like the sorcerer than the poor, frightened apprentice.

TAKING DISNEY AROUND THE WORLD

Michael agreed publicly that his reorganization of Disney had succeeded beyond even his wildest dreams. Privately, however, he felt that his plan of action was only just beginning to take effect. Now that the movie studios, theme parks, consumer products division, videotape sales, and record company were bringing in so much money, Michael had even bigger plans on how to invest that income to enlarge Walt Disney Company, as he renamed it. He wanted to make the company a *worldwide* entertainment conglomerate.

One of the ways that Michael Eisner has increased the sale of Disney consumer products is by the opening of company-owned Disney Stores, such as this one in Costa Mesa, California. (Alan Levenson/Time Magazine.)

Consumer Products

Consumers are people who buy things, and consumer products are the items they buy. A good movie idea that includes interesting characters can lead to a host of consumer products, including dolls or action figures based on the movie's characters, T-shirts with slogans from the movie, new drinks or snack foods inspired by the film, and everything from frisbees to plastic cups to camping tents decorated with pictures of the movie characters.

Often, sales of consumer products will earn more money for a company than the original movie earned. For example, the money earned from the sale of Mickey Mouse hats, T-shirts, cups, notebooks, stuffed animals, and other consumer products has long ago outstripped the earnings from the cartoons themselves. That's why, when a new movie comes out for children, there are likely to be all kinds of objects related to it for sale. These products often earn back a large part of the cost of the movie, and more!

Expansion in Japan and Europe

Already, Disney had sold its television cartoons and its new series, *The Disney Sunday Movie,* to TV networks across Europe. A Disneyland had been built in Tokyo, Japan, and Disney cartoons were

Disney "Imagineers" (artists and engineers) at work on a model of EuroDisney before its opening in the spring of 1992 outside of Paris. (Alan Levenson/Time Magazine.)

being broadcast as far away as China. Consumer products, including Mickey Mouse T-shirts, radios, and stuffed animals, could be seen around the globe. Now Michael planned to open a new theme park just outside Paris, France.

The park would be called EuroDisney and would closely resemble the original Disneyland in California. However, there would be a few added touches, including a bigger, more realistic European-style castle at the park's center and appropriate foreign languages spoken at the various pavilions. Michael was convinced Europe would welcome a Disneyland of their own, because **polls** taken at California's Disneyland and Florida's Disneyworld told him that Europeans were visiting those parks by the thousands every year. EuroDisney, in Europe's own backyard, would encourage even more thousands of visitors to join in the fun, and would increase the market for Disney shows and products. Michael planned its opening for the spring of 1992.

Expanding Markets in the United States

Another way Michael dreamed of expanding Disney's scope was to find more ways of reaching different types of people in the United States. Now that Disney Studios' movies were once again loved by children across the country, Michael decided to allow Touchstone Pictures to make comedies that appealed more to young adults. Touchstone was also permitted to make movies, like *Scenes from a Mall,* that middle-aged Americans might like.

And to be sure he touched on the interests of minority Americans, Michael established an **intern** program at Disney for young minority screenwriters. The beginning writers worked under

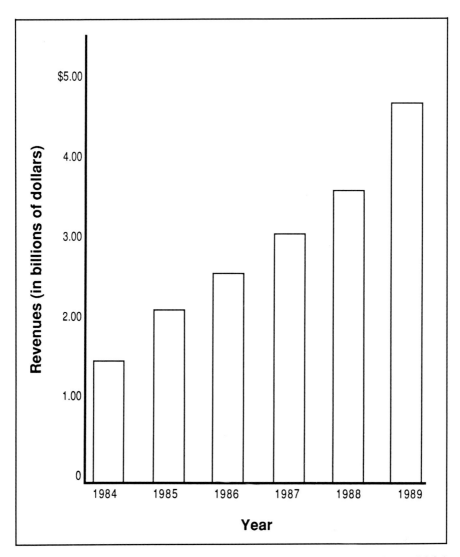

This chart shows the tremendous growth in Disney revenues from 1984 ($1.46 billion), when Michael Eisner became the company's chief executive officer, through 1989 ($4.59 billion).

contract for Disney Studios, learning how to write movies while actually seeing some of their screenplays produced. In this way, the writers had the chance of a lifetime to succeed in their professions, while Disney profited from their energy and fresh new talent. Once again, Michael was trading a chance at stardom for the good stories he needed to make inexpensive, highly profitable films.

Disney Studios was certainly a good place for a young screen-writer to make a start. In 1989, Disney released more hit movies, including *Honey, I Shrunk the Kids* and *The Little Mermaid*. Box office earnings for the summer of 1989 were $15 million more than for the summer of 1988. Michael decided to add a third movie studio to his empire to produce twenty-two movies each year in the future. The music from *The Little Mermaid* was another success for Disney's record department, which every year sells half the children's records bought in the United States.

Meanwhile, Michael didn't forget his pet division, the American theme parks. By early 1990, the Dolphin and Swan Hotels had been completed at Disneyworld. Their strange, fanciful appearance, with enormous concrete dolphins frolicking about the Dolphin Hotel and spectacular swans decorating the Swan Hotel, captured the imagination of visitors to Orlando. The hotels were filled with guests from their opening day.

A MOVIE THEME PARK

And Michael's ideas for other Disney theme parks were also finally coming true. For a long time, he had dreamed of building a theme park based on the back lot of a movie studio (the area of a studio where pictures are filmed). The rides would be straight out of

Spectators gasp in amazement at one of the exhibits as they pass by on "The Great Movie Ride" at the MGM-Disney theme park in Florida, which opened in 1989 near Disneyworld. (Joseph McNally/Sygma.)

famous old movies, and visitors would get to experience some of their favorite special effects—like an attack from a man-eating shark or a ride on a runaway train—in what looked like real life. On May 1, 1989, Michael's latest dream came true when he opened the MGM-Disney theme park in Florida, near Disneyworld.

The combination movie studio, tour ride, and thrills-and-chills excitement was sold out from the beginning. It is sure to increase Disney's revenues many times over. People eager to know what stunt men do can see almost all the great stunts reproduced in "The Indiana Jones Stunt Theater." And one can meet all of the greatest stars—from Tarzan to the Wicked Witch of the West—on "The Great Movie Ride."

Encouraged by his success with the MGM-Disney park, Michael began planning a sea-oriented theme park in Long Beach, California, not far from Disneyland in Anaheim. Who knows? It wouldn't be surprising if, in the back of Michael's mind, plans for a Disneyland in China are already hatching.

Chapter 7

Dreams Can *Come True*

Of course, not everything at Walt Disney Company has been sprinkled with magic fairy dust. There have been problems, and not all of them have been solved.

TROUBLES IN NEVER-NEVER LAND

For one thing, Disney's almost unbelievable success has made the company seem too greedy and aggressive to some. Many Hollywood insiders laughed at Disney for filing lawsuits for **trademark infringement** against the owners of certain day care centers and even the producers of the Academy Awards, who used Disney characters without permission.

The head of MCA Studios felt that Disney stole the idea for its movie theme park in Florida from him. And certain directors of

Trademarks

Anytime you see a little ™ or a tiny "R" in a circle marking a product or its package, it means that product—whether it's a soap or a soup or a cartoon character—has been trademarked. A trademark means the company that owns the product is the only company that can legally make or use or profit from that item. For example, the character of Sleeping Beauty in the Disney movie belongs to the Walt Disney Company, and no one else may use that character without Disney's permission.

At the Academy Awards ceremony one year, an actress dressed as Disney's Sleeping Beauty performed onstage. Disney threatened to sue the Academy Awards because the company had not given permission for the character to be used.

Disney threatened to sue because the Disney people felt that if Sleeping Beauty had behaved unpleasantly, that would hurt the character's image and she would become less valuable to the company. Other reasons to insist on a trademark include making sure no one else makes money by selling the owner's product, and having control over the quality of the product itself.

An artist works on the Wicked Witch of the West, another of the exhibits on "The Great Movie Ride" at the MGM-Disney theme park in Florida. (Joseph McNally/Sygma)

Disney films felt bullied when company executives constantly visited their movie sets to be sure they weren't overspending.

Growing Too Large

Another problem was that, as Disney grew bigger and became more profitable and more famous every day, fewer actors, directors, and writers were willing to work for them for low pay. This meant that Disney was no longer able to make low-budget movies. Thus, the profits from their movies were likely to shrink.

Relationships among the various Disney departments also became more difficult as the empire enlarged. Arguments broke out over which department should pay to develop certain ideas. Team Disney became too large to maintain its old, friendly, "team" atmosphere all the time.

There were also some disappointments in the products themselves, of course. Though the recent movie, *Dick Tracy,* made a profit, it wasn't nearly as much as the Disney people had expected. And the action figures inspired by its characters didn't sell well at all.

On the other hand, as one Disney executive philosophically put it, "There are limits to how big the pie can get." Out of the thirty-six films Disney made between 1984 and 1989, twenty-eight have made money. This may be the best winning streak for any movie studio, ever. Can Michael keep up the good work forever?

Luck Plays a Role

Of course, luck has played a big part in Michael's success. He was lucky that there were so many children being born just as he took over at Disney—children whose parents wanted them to rediscover Disney's magic.

Michael was also lucky that the American economy was booming just as he arrived on the scene. Videotapes were a brand new market, and the Disney company had an enormous reserve of products it could sell.

But all of these advantages existed years before Michael arrived at Disney. However, it took Michael's imagination, self-confidence, and sheer hard work to make the sum of the company earn more than its separate parts.

Sometimes, Michael's own crazy dreams have gotten in the company's way. Not all of his ideas for movies have been approved by the people he hired. But crazy dreams are what makes show business tick, and Michael Eisner has never been afraid to lay an idea on the table and see who gets excited. And he's made sure that if his ideas aren't "cool," his employees will be sure to tell him so.

WHAT WILL MICHAEL DO NEXT?

Michael Dammann Eisner has traveled far from his days of dreaming up stories about the strangers he watched on New York's sidewalks. But his imagination has never dimmed. And as everyone in Hollywood, even his enemies, is bound to agree: Michael Eisner loves a challenge.

"He's amazing," says one friend. He has the whole world asking, "Michael, what are you going to do next?"

The answer at Disney always is, "You ain't seen nothing yet."

Glossary

animation   Moving cartoons, like those in movies and on television.

asset   Property or other thing of value that belongs to a person or company.

bankruptcy   A legal declaration of an inability to pay debts.

blockbusters   Movies that earn over $100 million in ticket sales.

bottom line   The total amount that something costs, including even the smallest expenses.

capital   Money or goods that can be used to produce an income.

cash flow   The movement of money through a business, as when funds received for goods or services are used to pay debts.

chief executive officer   The highest office in a company.

conglomerate   A group of companies tied together into one large unit.

contract   A legal agreement; a person under contract agrees to work for a company for a certain period of time for a certain amount of money, and the company agrees to pay that person according to the agreement.

economy   The financial state of the country.

financing   Providing money for something.

grossing   The amount of money something earns, without subtracting the amount it cost in the first place.

income   Money earned from work, or from selling property or other things that are owned.

intern   A beginning worker who learns from someone who is more experienced.

invest   To spend money, time, or other resources in the hope of getting a larger amount back.

market   The group of people who will buy a certain product.

negotiator   One who bargains to reach an agreement with someone else.

patent   The right to be the only one to make, use, or sell a new invention for a certain number of years.

poll   A collection of opinions or facts on a particular subject.

prime time   The hours in the evening when more people watch television than at any other time—usually between 8:00 and 11:00 P.M.

profits   The amount of money made after all the costs of a project or business have been paid.

program director   The person who decides which television shows will be broadcast by a television network or station.

revenues   The money that is made from property or other investments.

theme parks   Amusement parks designed around a central idea, or theme; Disneyland is a theme park designed around Disney's cartoon characters and movie plots.

trademark infringement   Using a trademarked product without permission of the product's owner; trademark infringement is against the law.

Index

ABC Television, 10, 17–19, 20–23
American Safety Razor Company, 16

Baby-boom generation, 13–14, 18–19,
   28, 36, 38
Breckenridge, Jane (wife of Michael
   Eisner), 20

Captain EO, 35, 40

Denison University, 16, 17
Diller, Barry, 19, 22, 23–24
Disneyland, 9, 11, 30, 33, 35, 36, 45
Disney, Roy, 27
Disney Studios, 9, 31–32, 38–39,
   51, 53
Disney, Walt, 9, 10, 11, 27, 28, 36,
   41–42
Disneyworld, 9, 11, 30, 33, 36, 43,
   45, 53
Dolphin Hotel, 43, 53
Donald Duck, 36

Eisner, Michael,
   ABC-TV, 17–23
   birth, 13
   children, 29, 36
   dreamer, 7–9, 60
   education, 15, 16, 17
   marriage, 20
   Paramount Pictures, 23–24
   parents, 15, 16
   Walt Disney Productions, 25–60
Epcot Center, 11, 30, 33, 43
EuroDisney, 50–51

Fedder, Ted, 17

Graves, Michael, 43

Jackson, Michael, 35

Lucas, George, 35, 43

Market share, 14–15
McDonald's, 43
MGM-Disney (theme park), 55
Mickey Mouse, 9, 37, 46
Mount Kisco, New York, 13

NBC Television, 17

Paramount Pictures, 9, 10, 23–24
Park Avenue, in New York City, 7, 16

Ratings, 20–21

Star Tours, 35, 39–40
Swan Hotel, 43, 44, 53
Syndication, 40

Theme parks, 9, 11, 33–37, 40, 53–55
Topolino (magazine), 37
Touchstone Pictures, 31, 38, 39, 51
Trademarks, 56, 57

Walt Disney Company, 47
Walt Disney Productions, 9–11, 25–60
Wells, Frank, 26, 28, 29, 42

J.
B.

3743
$12.95

Tippins, Sherill
Michael Eisner : fun for
everyone

DATE DUE	BORROWER'S NAME	

IMPERIAL PUBLIC LIBRARY
P.O. BOX 307
IMPERIAL, TX 79743